voices from the void

voices from the void

Richard A. Donin

Radon Press

voices from the void

Copyright ©2003 by Richard A. Donin.
All rights reserved. This publication, or parts thereof, may not be reproduced in any form by photographic, electrostatic, mechanical, or any other method for any use, including information storage and retrieval, without written permission from the publisher.

Published in 2005
Library of Congress Control Number: 2003092290

Donin, Richard A. 1947 -
voices from the void: a collection of poems spanning several years of work.

For more information, contact:
Radon Press
PO Box 80653
Portland, Oregon 97280-1653
em: rdonin@m3productions.com

First Edition
Printed in United States of America
ISBN 0-9729205-0-1

To life...
and to the people
who have put up with me.

ACKNOWLEDGEMENTS

I want to thank my family and friends for their love, support, and inspiration plus those who kindled some of the words in this work. A very special thank you goes to Ms. Kay Ice, my editor, for all her thoughtful suggestions, wisdom, and patience in guiding me through this adventure.

I also want to thank Ms. Karen Pyle for her wonderful artwork that brings a rich visual interpretation of the poems to life, Mr. Tim Oakley of Oakley Design Studios for the graphic design, and Ms. Cheryl Dillard for her photography.

INTRODUCTION
As a child, pure feelings encompassed me, often too many at once. Sometimes this was overwhelming as waves of emotion from anyone nearby washed over me. For a time, I tried to duck their impact, hoping the onslaught would stop. When that failed, I tried to have only "good" feelings, or at least those that parents and society said were good. Finally I retreated completely to the safety of nothingness—no feelings, just action, movement, and the same smile. No matter what.

I dwelt in this place for a long time, and as payment for my rented space, I lost the ability to understand emotions on all but the most base level. I could not connect words to feelings because I had no personal point of reference. I was surrounded by an ocean of others' feelings—but my feet never got wet. This disconnection with self and others burdened me with the nagging belief that I was not very bright and a poor communicator. But not knowing what else to do, I stumbled off to college to earn an unidentified degree in the sciences.

Soon I found myself struggling with an English Comp assignment to write about one topic using different voices. I still remember sitting on a padded bench in the student union forty-five minutes before the assignment was due, angry at my predicament, lost in the panic of the moment. Then, a voice spoke with such clarity that words spilled onto the page as fast as I could scribble. Then another voice, completely different, told me a decidedly contrasting version of the same story. With five minutes to spare, I submitted the work. When the paper was returned, I was stunned by the praise. A very small part of me felt strangely satisfied.

A few years later, I was forced to take English Comp 303. Once again, I was stuck on an assignment, this time to write a paper about my "inner self," Oh god, I thought, what does that mean? Which part is "safe" to share? I sat isolated in class, surrounded by dozens of people writing god-knew-what. Then my hand began to write, the printing turning to cursive and then to all out scrawling. Out of utter turmoil popped *introspect*, the first metered poem I'd ever written. I was confounded by what felt real and silly at the same time, but it was, at that point, the clearest picture of inner me.

Several years passed, and my inner chaos was being continuously refueled by the pressures of relationships, work, and life. I could find no sanctuary, no quiet calmness, which I so desperately wanted. So I sought counseling, mostly just to make sure I wasn't truly nuts. It was a life-saving choice because I finally found the ability to listen to all of the inner voices.

Throughout this guided, sometimes hand-held, sometimes dragging-kicking-screaming-tearful encounter, internal voices spoke of experiences, giving me a rope bridge on which to begin the process of re-connecting to emotional well-being. Patterned by years of scientific method, I sought to classify, objectify, and catalog all of my newly discovered feelings. And, like in that English class, I felt compelled to write poems. But rather than metered rhymes, I chose a minimalist style to express and characterize observations, concrete yet fluid, engaging and intense, with power to impact and perhaps spark insight, bringing a small light to some darkness.

Generally, words exploded onto the page, prompted by emotional experience often beyond conscious thought, in some cases startling me with a voice I was hearing for the first time. Other words were purposely constructed, forming word dances. In several poems, the title is an integral part of the work, to be read as the first line of the poem.

In all, word placement as well as word choice has meaning. I strive for word paintings or visual, written sculptures—precise, compact, and sometimes austere—that capture the selected emotion as a frozen piece of time.

Each poem focuses on an awareness—of love, parenting, pain, depression, fear, or other life experience. Listening to the voices that allowed me to create these poems has been cathartic—often healing—for me; I hope that some of them may speak to you.

Richard A. Donin

TABLE *of* CONTENTS

voices from the void — 2

shadow of an instant...

introspect — 6
destiny — 9
summer breeze — 10
vision — 11
what to do — 12
the sight — 13
awakening — 15

etched upon my senses...

heartdance — 18
beauty — 19
you — 20
children — 21
alison and daniel — 22
vanished — 24
friend — 26
ivan — 27
grateful — 28
what you do to me — 29
soul mate 1 — 30
obsession — 32
soul mate 2 — 33
hearts — 35

mist	36
aura	37
flight	38
whispered image	39

crevasse of choice...

analogy 1	42
decisions	43
indecisions	45
pinnacle	46

silent spiral...

whirlpool effect	49
lost hope	50
glimpse	51
vincent	52
siege	53
missing	55
the child	56
gasp	58
finding my way	59

chill blanketing the spirit...

infected	63
needs	64
divorce	65
dreams	67

closer to clarity...

chaos	71
trust	72
prattle	73
lonesome	74
stress	77
the highway	78
the hunt	80
eggshell ballet	82
incredible lateness of being single	83
feelings	85
bliss	86
passion	87
emotion 1	89
emotion 2	90
analogy 2	92
analogy 3	93
ode to a wrong number	94
parenting	95
train	96

suspended in a sigh...

frustration	100
guilt	101
lonely	102
zen proverb	103

voices from the void

voices from the void

subdued chatter
real conversations
just beyond recognition

in a bottle
without sides,
cuneiform imprints
paper cannot grasp
inscribes past

worlds of wisdom skim by
speed reading slight of hand
astound my presence
touches present

abstract collage flows in 35mm
illuminates the darkness of daylight
caught behind my eyes
blinds remaining vision
radiates future

frustration motivates
driven to discover
message perched
on the tip of mind.

is this where inspiration
truly comes from
pulling me write or
is it the wind between my ears?

sometimes i wish they would
shout or shut up
so i can find moments peace
the loving rest of silence.

shadow of an instant...

introspect

other winds now lead the way
along the roads i used to play,
my only wish i'll never find
to give one thing for all mankind.

scribbled words half filled by ink
the sour milk i had to drink
deserted house with rotted beams
the blanket made of tattered seams.

aspirations held on high
reaching up to touch the sky,
shattered like the falling rain
upon a crumpled window pane.

a powerless, penniless man it teams
a patchwork make of broken dreams,
now locked against the bitter cold
on a lonely oregon road.

but through my walter mitty haze
my mind can clearly see those days
too old for everything, it's done,
gee i'm glad to still be young.

yet senseless reverie they say
will only make you waste the day,
and brainless, insane plots abound
to eyes not heed of public's frown.

so i'll follow foolish dreams
and try those stupid, crazy schemes,
sailing seas of discontent
never having to lament:
god i wish i'd done that.

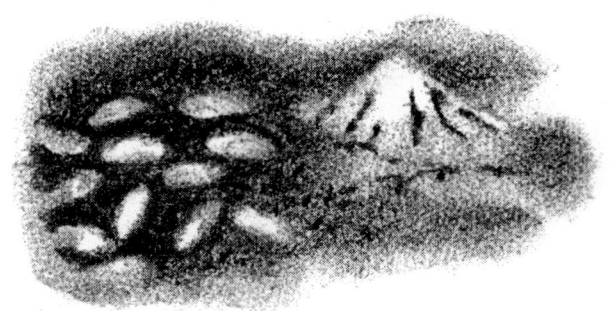

destiny

destiny

a puzzle,
no box
clue
pattern
nor rules.

pieces,
luminous
identical
absent distinct edges
fit only one way.

my map
my future
refuses rushed
completion.

belief as guide
each step
sightless progress
slowly reveals the
panorama.

summer breeze

nymph's whisper
    floats,
        gently directed,
            enchanting daydreams
to appear.

vision

within the shadow
of an
      instant
flows an
infinity called
      tomorrow.

what to do

when you've
recognized that
only   one
youthdream
remains.

possibly a definition of
transition?
beats me. but that
does not compensate
for the gothic matte
as mental tapestry
restlessly banging
in the wind.

is this tragic
foreshadowing
nearing end
or…
what to do.

for the longest time
i wanted to be-feel
artist.
it's my last one.
perhaps i dreamed too small
should have gone for a 100 lifetimes.

the sight

it returns,
always the same.

old man,
bitter and lonely
fondling his cane
perched upon
the park bench

staring into
himself.

awakening

awakening

impatient for coalescence
excitement grows
convergence grinds through
granite

months ago,
i thought, transmutation
was not possible

current tingles inside me
with a desire to
be free

well it should,
the struggle
has taken 46 years

chrysalis crumbles
to discover the
evolutionary step
has come
to me.

etched upon my senses...

heartdance

we waltz
spiritmusic flowing
floating, toes barely touching
ground
surrounded by cool dreammist,
apparition is sweet reality
lips pressed, tongues entwined
caressing
the scent of love.

warm skin slides
dark onto light
fusing
feeding
symbiotic nourishment
tingles head to toe.

this is how we will be.

beauty

gaze at the rose
see into the irises
understand their joy
and know
these creations are nature's
poor attempt at
a reflection of
you.

you

    a stylus glides across
        sentient silver,
  chemistry delicately engraves
        your spirit.

    a brush softly floats
        to paper,
  watercolors flow, effortlessly blending
        into your image.

    you are etched upon
        my senses
  a painting within
      this soul.

children

born of pistil and anther
dust of divergent novae
sparkles in their eyes,
evokes wonder and light
each touch, sight, smell, sound
a tiny incremental key hole
to the universe.

their garden nurtures
explosive growth,
changes our eyes and
mind cannot follow
we have been dulled into
snapshot awareness.

they are trillium
rare and brief
beauty exceeding
speech
a single breath
in the pattern of existence.

could that i slow time,
reverse it temporarily,
selfishly wanting them
to be as they were
my babies
all to myself.

mired in peter panisms
my face runs wet happiness
for i have been blessed.

alison and daniel

i knew who you were
in that instant of conception
girl and boy
the color of your hair
joy of your smile.

we share the magic of
the future and
the wisdom of the past
locked together by the
voice of the truth within.

i am blessed to
know how you feel
hear you think
touch what lies inside.

i leave you with the best of
me
vision, creativity,
a sense of wonder
without prejudice
the courage to risk,
to do it your way.

with open mind,
clear conscience,
follow your heart
it will not mislead,
your love and faith in
self
will support you through
everything.

as you stretch and grow
so will my love for you,
take the path of
unconditional love,
never look back.

believe in yourself
as i believe in you
for you will succeed
beyond your dreams.

love, daddy.

vanished

innocently exuberant smilelaugh
your thoughts transparent
vivid technicolor dreams
bridging to alternate reality.

sparkling joy eyes
brimming with thrill of
new experience rushes
no longer gasps for rollercoaster air.

grey, somber sorrow
hangs tousled blueblack
suit of quiet suffering
face mask seldom changing.

where are your dreams
those idea-notions
propel the imagination
through deepest sleep.

are they slumbering as well
or hiding behind the fearpain tree
maybe hanging from a just-coping-vine
perhaps running too fast to catch.

no longer i hear them
sight cannot chase them
may only surmise them
making worry over them
grow.

i must listen
show-me-the-way
back to your clear channel station
to emerge reconnected
via hearts and hugs.

remember you needn't
walk the path-not-taken
alone
i've been hiking there, too,
i am here, Daniel.

dad

friend

adamantine skies
youthful gleam
softly caresses
my child, my truth.

behind those eyes
lay such passion
     intensity
     artistry,
serene keen wisdom.

fragile orchid,
to the unaware
your form veils
elegant strength,
fierce independence.

sweet tranquillity,
poetic grace
reveals rare faith
in spirit self.

all that is you
beckons me
with warmth, safety
and the promise
     of love.

ivan

village elder
sits, dispassionate
hearing beyond words
seeing past the present

vast toolbox of
uncolored articulation tied
to measured responses
supportive and caring

you coax elusive candor
as insight gleams only
when disturbed by
my truth

father teacher confessor
emotional sculptor
silhouettes awareness
as i walk uncharted
into myself

i was fortunate to
find you and
this life you saved,
forever my thanks

on the next road
the roles may reverse,
i will remember.

grateful

small and common
overused, empty
utterance;
    dangles
        limply
on the tongue.

symbols used
no substance
of self
meaning, no feeling
yet i do!

lost.
so little for so much
seems
        unequal.

found.
from my soul
thank you.

what you do to me

your existence
pierces
my deafness
with music,

your presence
penetrates
my blindness
with color,

your being
fills
my experience
with passion,

your vitality
permeates
my emptiness
with spirit,

your reality
supplants
my discord
with meaning,

your life
restores
my psyche
with reason,

without you,
survival has
no music, no color,
no passion, no spirit,
no meaning, no reason.

soul mate 1

i am
    a flame
coolly sparkling,
igniting the embers
of your spirit.

    a breeze
arranging words to flow
like music, charming
your inner light.

    a butterfly
dancing on gusts
as fabric in the wind,
born of the joy within.

    a landscape
awaiting to fill our
canvas, returning
your sight to the future.

    a sea
tireless and constant,
a sweet, caressing rhythm
between your thighs.

a universe
spinning questions,
to match your answers
with unconditional love.

a rainbow
of feelings capped by a
sprinkle of stardust,
joined to you through eternity
your soul mate,
forever,
i am.

obsession

single image
elbows in front of
consciousness
shouting pushing shoving
its ever widening girth
blocks my window of clarity
beats up reason beyond
recognition,
hearing ceases.

a pinch in our recipe
makes us motivated
dedicated
tenacious
successful.

mixed with you
a staggering force
unbalances creation and
the matrix of reality.

you are all,
little else matters
entangled
attached
nature's super glue
has no solvent
nor i the want of such.

soul mate 2

your scent caresses
warm and soft
as petals in a vase

your touch resonates
tingling and strong
as music to the ear

your image moves
vibrant and beautiful
a living Renoir

you are the sculpture in my soul
the desire within my senses
the love of my life.

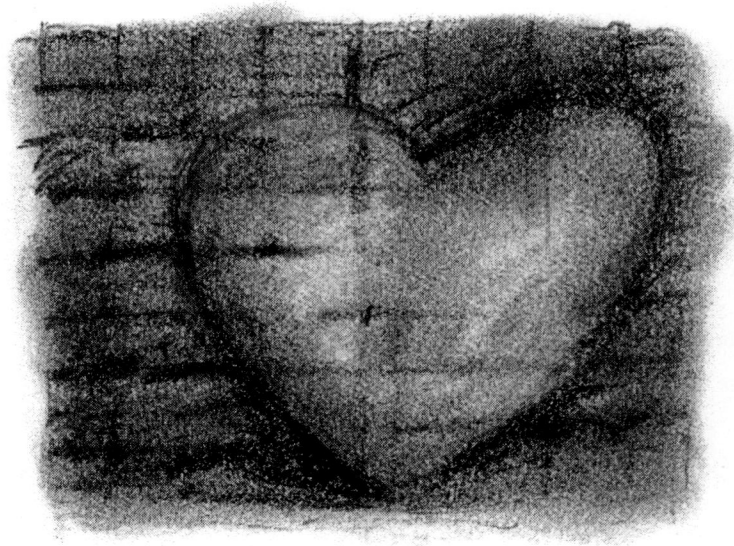
hearts

hearts

each breath
                hangs
anchor hitting bottom
well of pain intensifies as
relationship shatters

we lock away our hearts
in fear
wishing not to be
carried away in
the chariot of desire
to end up
mired in that dismal
desert of splintered chests

amid the terror
loneliness becomes
acceptable
dulled as survival

it is not right,
safety deposit
box life style

cardiac muscle must stretch,
be given and lost,
for the joy of love
is far greater than
the grief of
rejection.

mist

love as the
dew
spans a crystal second

descending gently,
cool
shallow breath
veils harsh edges
as soft tones
whisper
time's passage.

aura

upon bounce world
grows red snow
cocoon sun woman,
sea blue topaz sparkle eyes
illuminates
wet magic song
born of starlight
passionheat.

flight

    i float at
    the edge
                you
    lead not to an
    abyss, but
    flight
    soaring/throbbing/rhythmic
    heat
    which this rare
    love
                commands;
    even distance
    bows in awe
    as two
    as never before
    are
    one.

whispered image

translucentsoft
zephyrus stirs
alphabets
shaped into
language,

same picture, always
pouring from your
lips
awakens my focussed
consciousness.

voice ignites
fallingquickly into
pants
becoming joy,
smile and laugh.

you fuel a
shared harmony of
connection
very few experience
as i.

crevasse of choice...

analogy 1

bafflement mocks,
jabberwacky crow.
expanding contradiction
engulfs,
        consumes
the ultimate parasite
dies
        to live again
        within the crevasse
        of choice
never-ending.

decisions

even the little
puddles
everyone else
jumps over with ease
strike my chord of
terror,
i can't swim.

decisions

the grand canyon is
no match
for the gaping
pit
where my stomach
used to be.

decisions

are oft based upon
indecision.

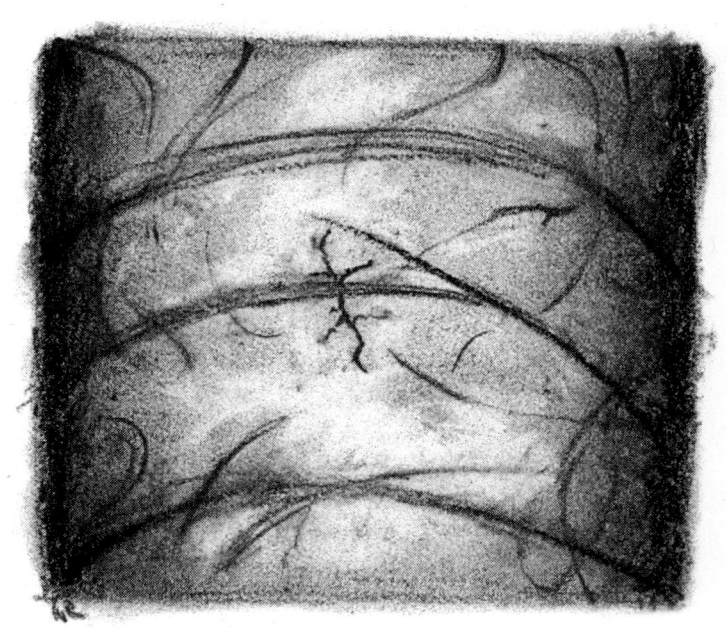

indecision

indecisions

mental roadblocks
forbidding movement,
leaves one standing
firmly in
emotional quicksand.

indecisions

expanding fissure divides
the conscious with leaving
few vines to span the
crossing
with no return.

indecisions

the trick is to
pick up that first
vine before the
beast attacks.

indecisions

drain your batteries
and leave no
jumper cables.

pinnacle

the height of
indecision,
getting drunk
at the
veritable quandary.

silent spiral...

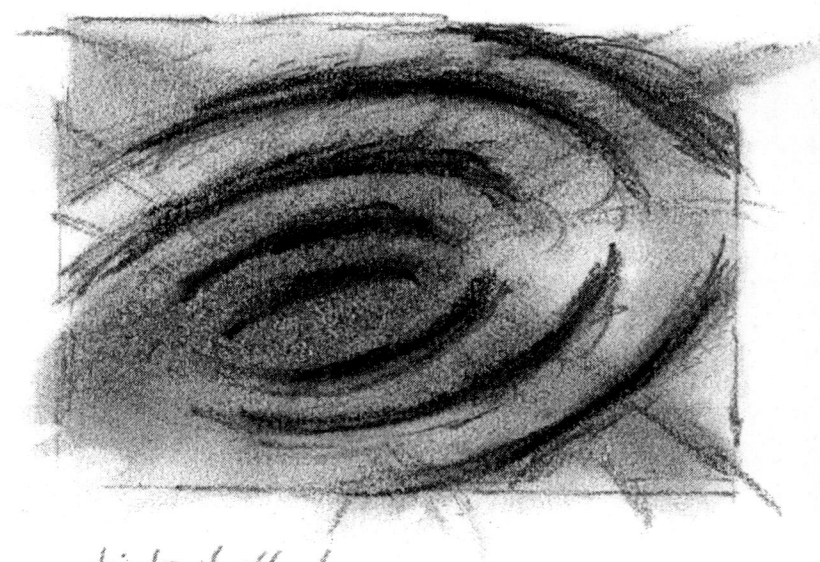

whirlpool effect

whirlpool effect

...depression,
a silent spiral
reaching inward,
untouchable;
my helplessness—
a tear is shed,
and i, too, am bound...

lost hope

drowning
in my
thoughts

i toss
myself
a life preserver

just beyond
my
reach.

glimpse

i saw you in me
willy loman
and you know,
you weren't insane.

it's all perspective.

your motives were
all right,
your means were incorrect.

automobiles, willy
are much too
messy.

vincent

you were fortunate,
at the time
    it never seemed so.

your legacy beyond
measure, a spirit
pigment captured,
your vision translated
whorls on canvas.

you searched fields, cities
and skies to find the
antidote to emptiness
feeling more abandoned
by each stroke.

staring into your mirrored
tunnel of darkness,
blanks the eyes as
your hand records it,
despite the horror.

were i so lucky.
i share the madness
    without the gift.

we liked each other,
our shared sin of intensity
common ground,
perhaps we'll meet again.

siege

caught between a vice of screams
resounds a battle's din,
the phrases burst as words assault
this conflict from within.

a bugle's ululation stabs
from ruins filled with tears,
as dust so slowly sets upon
those bunkers built of years.

the message has been written
and so it soon shall be,
my wants and needs prepare retreat
for the day i will not see.

missing

missing

rolling over
my hand lands
empty
to where you should be.

the pattern repeats
first wonder,
then loss,
finally pain.

emotion grows
slow motion
in my sleep until,
with shocking force
i am awakened.

where are you, better,
where am i?
turning against the
sorrow, i have no
energy for sleep.

the child

centuries of broken hearts
oppress esprit
returning to this place
whenever abandoned
by her love.

inner boy's
distress
overwhelms rational
behavior, such confusion,
no longer confident to
guide my own.

embroiled
unable to care take
lost amid kept
history of sorrow.

perhaps i'm incapable of
parenting and loving
at these times so
barren, little left
to give.

rancid cream
fear and
inadequacy
rise to the top
curdling all else inside,
depression is upon me
walls are forming.

having been here before,
must i be destined to live
this bleak hell
carved by mea culpa?

noiseless voice
inflicts unseen wounds,
sadly over
practiced at self-mutilation,
seemingly,
too fragile to be in love.

gasp

engine running on
fumes
burrowing
gnawingknowing
    empty
conjugated as
    lonely
has come to defile
what could be.

    wearied
cloak conceals
fire against
lack of it,
plays
emotional chameleon
to an audience of
    i
breeds unhappiness
    need to change.

passion's radiance
must fill me
    survival
        is not enough.

finding my way

wrapped in a robe
of sorrow
the view has altered
my trajectory.

a stained mirror
i behold
replaces the
intuition i seek.

hands of control
refuse cognizant
commands,
years of use
implanted as instinct.

i battle for release
fail surrendering,
to move beyond
turn cloak to smoke
anguish to understanding.

chill blanketing the spirit...

infected

failure's gray grime disease
covers with a chill
blanketing the spirit
as it searches for the
crack
in one's pride
to enter.

the dust devil of ambition
offers no mercy as it
multiplies, exponentially,
from within,
for entrapped ego
recovery degenerates into
escape.

as the internal ash storm builds
it blocks the light of
reason,
the pathogen
unknowingly destroys
all.

needs

necklace of culture
common pearls
of essentiality
joined by
psychological bond
delicately connected
interdependent,

fail helplessly
when, under tension
lacking emotional sustenance,
the string is broken

they fall towards a
shattered
lifedream.

divorce

a siren's song
two voices call
unyielding, so strong,
pull fate's chord
and change two lives
mere puppets
no reply.

the loudest shout
of rage may win
as compassion is thrown out
usurped by retribution
making vengeance
paramount.

yet each is clear
these tunes within
beckoning history to appear
as dread, that giant,
trudges on crushing
landscape built of years.

caught between the pull
of broken record's play,
vows crash against the shoal
at barrister's low ground,
a tag team match from hell
is jihad's lasting goal.

dreams

dreams

    tiny bits of torn
    paper float
    ever so gently
    until, they are

    impaled

    by reality
    upon the

    ground.

closer to clarity...

chaos

chaos

its existence
in webster
proves nothing
definable.

an excuse in
misconception
surrounded by auras
of inaccuracy
forced into category
where no box exists.

slightly out of focus
singularity in motion,
changing at random
belies the truth
it permeates.

reacting in fear
at mere mention,
minds of limited
understanding grapple
the googol exceeding bounds
of intellect
not based in holistic
reference.

before there was time
chaos lived
wise and laughing,
knowing,
it is of us
and we are it.

trust

spun web
fragile and precious
shiny and pure

until;

as water to steel
unguarded,
without the work of
care;

erodes to but a small
residue
  rust.

prattle

ah me,
incessant jay,
full of thoughtless
squawk,

battling my demons
oblivious to others
destroying more
than i comprehend,

payment will be
demanded.

lonesome

great pellucid cloud
loneliness
washes round the globe
not wet pools brimming
empty hearts

eddies portray
small children of
no loving adult
exploitpredation
swirls next to

hopeless teens
losing the wonderment
caught in trends beyond their
 control
childadult

current pulls, again,
upon those
not knowing whom they are, where
to go
adultchild

falling into
growing group
new to grayswimming
liquid mid-life
anxious and aging

tide's grasp netting many
moving toward the edge of
existence
awash in unfulfilled dreams
endlessly circling

all have surrendered
to tears.

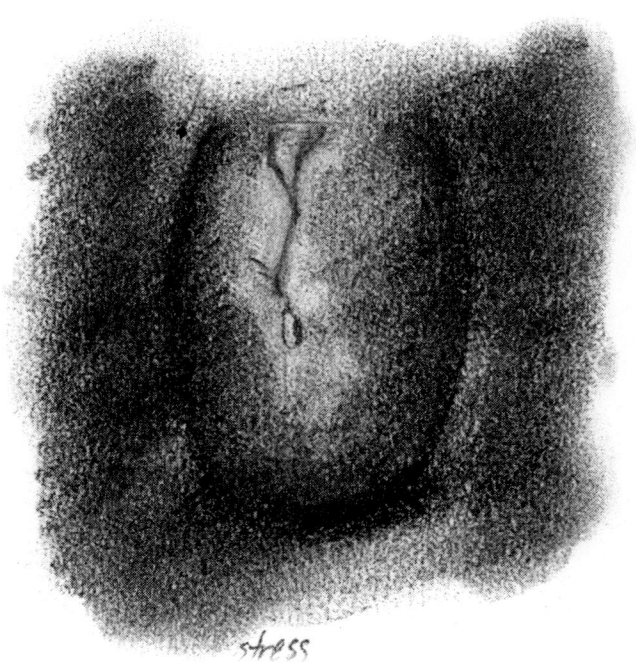

stress

he sits,
like the kernel of
popcorn,
trapped,
awaiting the inevitable.

the sheath that faithfully
excluded the elements
is now his downfall.

amid the heat and strain
the seed
utters but one
final sound.

alas,
no one looks
closely to see
the teardrop.

the highway

it's night again
windshield grimy
baggage stowed
gas tank barely
half full

speeding past
tundra memories
in the distance
headlights, tale lights

road suddenly veers
      tires squeal passing
      opportunities only to be
      remembered
as stupidity

one lane left
ferrari doesn't notice my glance
again i dream
windshield tint changes

pull over for a wash
foolishly thinking the
exterior all that matters
as more baggage gained

re-filled, back to speed
another search
more choices
new lines
time to dare
i ask directions

replace the glass
amid realization
my fantasies
deplete the fuel and
speed the drive
going nowhere

look past the trim line
into the driver as
she looks into me
moving toward tandem
with untested skills

no madness
desperation
only chemistry of
motion tied to
openwill hearts

the highway beckons
call drowned out
by internal song
parked in
harmony.

the hunt

three million years
scarred into male
collective
essence
binds us to
outmoded paths

big cat
skillfully silent,
senses
the moment
mate prey
is unaware

psyche being
self, wraith
frozen in our dna
holds back advancement

useless hidden agenda
constipates the present
forces lies
befuddles trust

anachronism
displaces the future
in pointless discussion;
men still think with
their smallest organ

such a waste,
the hunter
stands quivering
on the landfill of
extinction.

eggshell ballet

time lapse spin
holding your breath
slow
      sidestep
eyes cast down

pas de deux
mired in weighted
syllables

communication's edifice
mangled shards of silence
fill the horizon
touched by foreboding

for sometimes
it seems like
any
relationship
is better than none at all

this cannot be truth
merely
fear of the
unknown
disguising itself
as rationality

the grace is deafening,
dance no more
i must sit down.

incredible lateness of being single

finality's shock has
set-in
so long since feeling this
alone

imbalance overwhelms
old confidence
no match for the mirror

wisdom of the moment
turns chalky and difficult to
swallow
i must backstep
into unfolding
old panic

having been there
you'll ask
why so long to
move

be kindloving
and
breathe

you're making it.

feelings

feelings

they come again,
calling,
blinking confusion
outside my reasoning
they lack boxes i was told.

moving resonance
of foreign language,
scattered interpretation
rhyme without meaning
caught as unconnected
words and phrases,
i tremble at consequences
outside understanding.

hiding,
invisible to my search
beyond my seizure
energy dispersed throughout,
impressions traveling
outward from my core
affect all with
stunned reality.

their power shapes
actions and thoughts,
simple words of
imprecise process
untrained, unprepared
to join tides of self
to oceans of emotion,
i surrender in their grasp
no closer to clarity
only reaction.

bliss

>you are one
>>step
>closer
>to
>being there,
>when you've
>stopped running
>>from yourself
>as the reason for
>running
>>to anything else.

passion

the essence of
  lifeforce
a symphony in
stardust
woven throughout
existence

invisibly
colors our perception
brings design to
chemistry's timeless
interplay as
meaning to the
inanimate
stimulates joy
imagination
and truth

ever expanding
all possibilities
blossom as
light
for there is no
vacuum
only the fluid of its
essence.

emotion

emotion 1

brother fear
taps the shoulder
grabbing your hand
pulls you
      descending
      into the lurid
      recesses within one's
      psychic dungeon

      never to return

the same.

emotion 2

from clenched teeth
through the back of my jaw,
to the center
of my diaphragm
it is borne,

spawned by
resentment
fueled by
indignation
prodded by entitlement
it grows, feeding upon itself

coalescing,
the mass moves
dominating reason
pummels the boundary
of self control
straining to fission into
spewing screaming
rage

destructive brew
sanctifies my righteousness
gives purpose to
my fury

you, as i, know
it is home to
blame and hate
the place where
violence arises,
anger.

analogy 2

wisp of apollyon laughter
as senses blend and fade
to a throbbing fog awareness
its geometric intensity
infects the mind
with no room for thought.

reduced to instinct
any escape is just
as animal action takes control
the body races
out distancing all presence
on a parabolic path of sweat.

the darkness decays
as the present fuses slowly
restoring self;
never to remember
the encounter,
but for the word
pain.

analogy 3

he is near.

relentless;
silent hunter
moves without pity
in eternal pursuit
having never missed.

the odor.

lingering shadow
of precise aim
unseen spear
breaks a time line
and the journey to dust
begins.

ode to a wrong number

impersonal fool
yet mother lets it be,
for whom the bells toll
words cannot feel.

i race,
wrong time,
alarm at night
strangles one's breath
with conditioned heed

stumbling
my heart speeds
only to find
a misplaced finger.

man's tool
coiled to strike
has me in its grip,

oh mother
i wonder if you know;
pavlov was right,
alexander,
i wish you were in
my area code.

parenting

28 hour a day job
non-existent manual
no time clock punched

responsibility welded to
teaching unconditional love,
expressed in many ways

listening to their youth
being repetitive
consistent
smiling
laughing
crying

i can't believe there is
no formal training,
no learner's permit
so many on auto pilot
without a light

small wonder many
get it so wrong
unable to undo the past
themselves recovering children
continuing the abuse
neglect and shame

wake up fools!
your kids need you
as adult not
competing with them
as child,
they know the difference!

train

memories of
shiny six crayon box color
paint upon hand crafted
wood, cotton cord fitted
with red wooden ball
to keep small hands from slipping,
so many smiles.

blue engine puffed
cerebral smoke illusory whistle
connected orderly empty open top box cars
rolled
smoothly,
caboose happily following.

no matter how fast i ran
gliding effortless pull
as black wheels turned,
blocks, treasures, stuffed
animal freight carried
around play room.

when did i trade those
soft toys for
phrase pictures and
chain of words?

all is in tatters
faded chipped wobbly
by the dozens
cars now full of
sorrow, mistakes, laments.

railroad of grief
stretches far behind
rope fused to shoulder
each lory brimming with
jumbled history cargo
quackgrass words sticking up
too visible in rear view mirror.

speed no more
aging weariness dragging,
desire swells
to unhitch load
returning to
sweet remembrance.

suspended in a sigh...

frustration

is part of the shock
of finding
cold water in the
hot tap of life.

guilt

    little balloon
        expands,
            pushing all
          else
                out of the

            way.

lonely

suspended in a
                    sigh
eternity waits
silent and
uncompromising.

old zen proverb

as the flower within us,
each child blooms
in its own time.